"I enjoyed these poems immensely."
– William Peter Blatty, author of *The Exorcist*

"Lucid, raw and honest poems, refrains that slide with grace and wit from the particular to the general, from past to present and back again, authentic and absorbing."
– novelist and screenwriter Rudy Wurlitzer (*Pat Garrett and Billy the Kid* and *Little Buddha*)

"If you ever get caught in the subway between stations, try to sit beside a guy like the guy who wrote these poems."
– novelist David Gilmour (*The Film Club, Back On Tuesday*)

"Funny and fun to read, playful but also deadly serious...a depth of experience got at only in the best poetry."
– novelist Samuel Thomas Martin (*This Ramshackle Tabernacle, A Blessed Snarl*)

AFTER HOURS

Library and Archives Canada Cataloguing in Publication

Epp, Darrell, 1972-, author
        After hours / Darrell Epp.
Poems.
Issued in print and electronic formats.
ISBN 978-1-77161-219-7 (paperback).--ISBN 978-1-77161-220-3 (html).--
ISBN 978-1-77161-221-0 (pdf)

        I. Title.
PS8559.P72A64 2016   C811'.6   C2016-901094-5
                                           C2016-901095-3

Published by Mosaic Press, Oakville, Ontario, Canada, 2016.

MOSAIC PRESS, Publishers

Copyright © 2016 Darrell Epp

Printed and Bound in Canada

Cover art by Gord Pullar

Designed by Courtney Blok

ONTARIO ARTS COUNCIL
CONSEIL DES ARTS DE L'ONTARIO
an Ontario government agency
un organisme du gouvernement de l'Ontario

We acknowledge the Ontario Arts Council
for their support of our publishing program

We acknowledge the Ontario Media Development Corporation
for their support of our publishing program

Funded by the   Financé par le
Government   gouvernement   Canada
of Canada   du Canada

MOSAIC PRESS
1252 Speers Road, Units 1 & 2
Oakville, Ontario L6L 5N9
phone: (905) 825-2130

info@mosaic-press.com

www.mosaic-press.ca

AFTER HOURS

By Darrell Epp

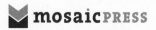

mosaicPRESS

Contents

Contents

Contents

Contents

'Life when one does my kind of work is rather strange.'

-William Butler Yeats

No Strings Attached

skateboarding down wellington trying to decide
between betty and veronica while nodding on
a line of chandler—*the passing minutes like
spent rockets*—and marveling at the summer
infestation of hawks, their shadows spattering
the sheraton as you come this close to finally
outrunning your past, starting clean. you yell
in triumph, skid along the curb, draw power
from the musky scents of passersby. some
pedestrians you recognize. nabokov
defined art as 'beauty plus pity' and
today has plenty of both, even if no
one notices and tattooed rage-boy
can't stop picking off the weak, the
fearful. there's nothing to fear. up
ahead they're riding jackhammers,
that looks like a fun job. kids laugh,
savor their first swear words, a man
kicks a parking meter and you'd love
to hug the whole downtown ward, it
doesn't matter how they feel about it.
the new mayor has big plans. wish him
well, salute his make-work projects:
rock gardens, high-rise parking lots,
flower beds, the languors of the
lilics, their spidery blossoms.

Strange Fruit

so i wound up in east tanganyika
(don't even ask) choking on
urgwagwa sitting at john wayne's
table in the impala hotel he filmed
hatari! there in 1966 i loved the
strange fruit the masai mutely
hawking jewelry by the roadside
the constellations lit up like vegas
neon hated the european tourists
the muzungu-this muzungu-that
and having to say apana asante to
hustlers all day long i went to the
picasso cafe ate burgers with a
backpacking australian we took
turns asking so what are *you*
running from his name was
even jonah you can't make that up
i was sick of being told not to waste
my potential so instead of winning a
nobel prize or an emmy i stared into
the sun until my visa expired odd
who you run into there freaks
romantic failures drunk geniuses
those blue-uniformed school kids
what was it they were saying
when they pointed at me and
laughed no one ever told me.

Balmoral Tavern

wind throws snow against the window.
far away the ice is cracking. the other
side of blue, a weary sort of bliss. this

is where i saw my first stabbing, this
is where i calculated the odds, hesitating
for years. certain physical constants

would check their hats at the door.
farther south than the emperors of
antarctica, grateful for a room where

hank williams still sang every night.
'the silence of a falling star lights up
a purple sky,' he'd cry, and it would

remind me of a word you used to say,
it rhymed with something else, what
was it now, almost got it, no, it's gone.

Benefits

in a weird camera obscura special
effect through translucent curtains,
dawn lurches forward like a truck

with stripped gears. tweeting like
a test pattern, sunlight refracts
through a million private prisms,

impaling flesh on spears of flame.
unemployment has its benefits.
i salute the early bird commuters,

the way they boost the country's
gross national product, but right
now i'm more concerned about

the trapezoidal shadows dancing
impishly atop your perfect pelvis.

Looking West on Cannon St. East

it's that time of year; a freshwater breeze
drags junk mail and leaves past my stoop
and all the way to taco bell and beyond.

this used to be the classy part of town,
before electricity. these bricks are
older than the union jack!

seasons change.
the mayor forgets us.
absolution's out of town.

like conscripted grunts we carry on
with hard-won stoicism. farther
along, bronze tributes to our

pioneering forefathers: the macnabs
and mcmasters; robber barons,
sons of the gentry. we haggle

over dimes as, out in the harbour,
the future rests on her haunches
with an all-knowing smile.

your guess is as good as mine.

Sparks

stupefied ex-beauty queens
facebooking old flames.
husbands, freshly neutered,
mowing america's lawns.

the unspeakable realization
of futility, the superstitious
rabble with their pitchforks.
have a beer, read the paper.

circular logic, like after a
layoff. sweaty comedians
dying for a laugh. photons
like a shower of sparks,

jolting the extras back into
wakefulness. it doesn't last.
focus on the routine, forget what
you see when you close your eyes.

Weather Report

unnoticed, grace rolls in from the northwest,
raining down on rub-and-tugs and cemeteries,
the tenements with the asbestos and the live
wires, that rich duke's house they turned into
a museum, shawarma huts and money marts—
raining down on the just and unjust with no
questions asked. anil verma scratches to win
like his life depends on it; over his shoulder,
his shadow is laughing at him. moishe gets
tagged by the new red light cameras, adrian
thinks of going back to school for something
practical and when things get tight everybody
stares into a glowing screen, we have at least
that much in common. dean's on his knees
again, hoping jesus grades on a curve. zero
per cent financing; half off; one day only.
it's raining harder now, down the graffiti-
stained plywood where the windows used
to be and something about how the walls
meet the roof makes me weepy, jittery.
something's up tonight; we tighten our
grip on our remote controls. grace comes
to town and we don't even hit pause as
it rains all the way to the erie canal and
down on a drafty row house sublet to a
sensitive soul, riding a crest of bad luck.
next to his toilet's a million-selling how-
to book called YOUR BEST LIFE NOW.
the author's incisors twinkle like stars.

The River

twitching waiting for the mailman
wondering about how things change.
'you can't step in the same river twice,
you said, because the river's constantly
changing. 'if that's true, i said, 'you
can't step in the same river even once,
can you? it's changing as you're stepping.'
but you didn't understand what i meant
and you certainly never understood how
much i wanted to build us a treehouse
in the jungle where we could eat bananas
all day and i could beat my chest like i
was tarzan lord of the apes. and what
were you thinking anyhow, glibly quoting
heraclitus to man with tears in his eyes?
like a dog returning to his vomit i patrol
the used bookstores, the empty cathedrals.
the sheets don't smell of you, like always.
how gone you are, how always returning.

Famous Last Words

can't explain, but if i could what would change?
would strangers salute me, or present me
with a gold-plated trophy, or the
unsmiling neighbour ignoring
me in the elevator, the guy
with the artificial leg, would
he—and everybody else,
maybe—truly and terminally
'get it'? would i become
the man who makes the
world's best omelet, the
'most improved, by far!'
at the high school reunion?
i feel my rage soften, melt
away, replaced by a
narcotic drowsiness. *can
you please tell me where i'm going?*
asks the tourist in the hawaiian
shirt, cowboy boots and hat
on his feet and head. ridiculous,
that much is obvious, but
there's always the last minutes
of *touch of evil*, always
marlene dietrich asking
the audience, i mean, me: what
does it matter what you say about people?

Times It By Seven

hazard lights winking at an inside joke,
fords hondas and toyotas from here to
where and i think i finally get it:

i loved too much or not enough,
unwise, unwell, the one-eyed
ogre with his necklace of skulls

or the bashful ghost running from
his shadow. opium-sweet agony
like a blizzard of hypodermics,

soul of a grub, rub-a-dub-dub,
photographs lost in the fire,
pink barrette, seed of a tooth,

sick rose, hungry worm, two,
now one, one, now gone: it
sounds even worse in dog years.

We Do What We're Told

for our convenience,
foreigners are tortured, caged.
we focus our gaze
on super bowls, the sales tax.

how fastidiously we wipe
the blood off the grand piano.
deathly worried about this or
that, we start a bonfire.

our kindling, sacred texts
and knotted femurs. save
the jewelry, the gold teeth:
there's talk of a recession.

let's go to the drive-in,
heartbroken king kong
is swatting down fighter
jets like they're fireflies.

let's hold hands in the
dark, ignore the ghosts
prowling the cornfields
like orphaned shadows.

Clean Break

i couldn't believe how far away everything was.
like an ill-fitting gorilla costume the decades
made my hair sweat, made me gasp for air.
and then some half-robot superhero
stepped on my foot and stole my cab,
made some joke about life insurance,
it's crazy what people get away with.
i thought of going to a motivational
seminar: alpha male? i'm barely a
delta male, ha ha etc. my roommate's
a scientist now, he slices up rat brains.
all of my exes teach kindergarten, i
wouldn't have the patience. children
it's time for finger painting is what
they say instead of i'm not getting
any younger, and what's your problem,
and i'd like to make this a clean break.

No Thank You

a sense of unspeakable frustration
ripples through the crowd when
the execution's postponed. the

firing squad's stuck in traffic.
we say we love justice but
we're really just bored. fire-

breathing sword-swallowers
retrained for data entry, baby
mermaids flushed down the toilet,

armani-clad satyrs prowling the
scene like they own it, cathedrals
reborn as abattoirs. dr. frankenstein

smiles for the cameras. he says
he's found the fountain of youth,
all that's missing is your credit

card, satisfaction guaranteed.
there are some souls even
hell doesn't want.

Dirty Tricks

the weather's been so crazy lately
i'm not even surprised
when my shadow packs its bags
and hitches a ride back to the
garden of eden.

a blizzard in a foreign language
has us searching for the candles,
doesn't even care that it's adam
and eve's wedding anniversary.

dirty tricks are played by
laws of nature, laws of story,
and i forget what else
until here i am planting

sunflowers in my beard,
missing my shadow and
worrying about the ants
who marked its movements
on their teeny tiny calendars.

Public Enemy

you recognize yourself on the post office wall
and your heart swells, you've never felt 'most
wanted' before, or wanted much at all. hard
to recall your crime but it's a good feeling,
like finally beating the rubik's cube two
summers after the fad had died off, the
fitness guru pulling a bus with his teeth,
the zoot-suited dictator cataloguing the
skulls of his enemies, gloating over
the strength of his zombie slave
army. 'the big thieves hang the
little thieves.' that's what your
polish grandma always said
and what would you expect
in a world made of spare parts
and iou's? you can't make gold
without exploding a star, what a
waste! you tire of being the villain,
maybe it's time to be a grunting
cave man or a good boy scientist,
curing diseases *pro bono*. tough
decision, but dorothee makes the
call: scientist it is. good boy.

Civil Disobedience

missing pieces, essential
to the production—
holding your hand at
the mouth of the erie
canal, for example.
the night we broke
the bed. grimly muttered
threats from a kick-ass
revenge flick: *how does*
it feel to be hunted, or
some similar nonsense.
i put recyclables in with
the regular garbage and
call it civil disobedience,
a form of defiance against
whoever's in charge. far
away there are mountains,
monkeys, elliptical galaxies
dancing unto death; the
knowledge of them, in
haunted parking lots,
providing more than
enough consolation.

Wish List

i wish this coffin had a sun roof.
i wish down was up, that would
be so helpful. i wish i could
believe you when you say
'your call is important to us.'
i wish i could fix
all the leaky buckets,
punch all the celebrities,
kiss all the babies.
i wish everybody told me i reminded
them of general george washington,
instead of the bizarro superman
(first appearance: superboy #68,
october 1958) who said hello
before leaving the room, who
cast his pearls before swine,
who beat his son with
a long leather strap
for coming home
with straight a's.

Darrell Epp

What In The World

...and whole neighbourhoods
fashioned out of a different
brand of molecule, it's all
dollar-store knockoff stuff
around here, a viral confusion
flitting from mind to mind,
an encroaching darkness like
God's shadow, i'm thinking
of henry fonda in *the wrong
man*, that over the shoulder
look on his face as he saw
his old life receding from
view, and he doesn't even
have to say what in the world
is going on here, you can just
tell, the joints age, crack and
pop like death's r.s.v.p., out
in the park, in the shade of
statues of forgotten war heroes.

Cherry Blossoms

discarded scratch-and-win lottery tickets
cartwheeling down barton st. e
(i wish they were cherry blossoms),
somehow further aggravating
the sweaty lassitude of july.

a sort of symmetry rolling in like a wave:
noumenal as childbirth, inevitable as
weather. history holds its breath.
random pigeons and squirrels
planning for the winter, i can

barely imagine tomorrow, the
discrete particles comprising
the ligaments of the day, the
world, its movers and shakers,
their suburban duplicitous daughters.

Contraindications

an unpolluted pacific

a garden of eden sky

the man in the moon

a star's molten heart

a volcano's teardrop

put one of the above under your
tongue every 4 hours or as needed.

do not mix with food. do not answer
the phone. and if anybody asks, tell

them you haven't seen me, tell them
you haven't seen me for months.

If I Wasn't So Selfish

the pages of richard's masterpiece were all blank.
empty white fields like virgin clouds, as
rothko said 'silence is so accurate,' he
was crying i was barely listening and
if i wasn't so selfish i would adopt a
pet, or maybe just a cactus. we could
watch her spines repel predators and
jehovah's witnesses, invite friends
over, teach them about photosynthesis.
we'd go to benin, dig holes for the
poor, bake pies, give expert advice
to lost travelers, enraged taxpayers
ripping up their maps, atoning in
vain for past sins, wrong numbers.
i lie, i'd get bored in a week, throw
her overboard for a coniferous shrub
or even just a leaf helicoptering on
autumn breezes down to the gutters.
like in 'the tortoise and the hare' i
cover less ground by speeding up,
say less than richard does by saying
nothing; there's nothing more to say.

Darrell Epp

Under New Management

rosa says she's too old to change and you can
take it or leave it, you two-faced fairies.
during her smoke break the whispers
come out, sharpened like daggers.

i cover both my ears, neutral as switzerland.
my cubicle doubles as a coffin, my life as
a long ride to the oncology waiting room.
where is here and why am i: the hell of

if if if. lily will be graduating in no time. my
ancestors were legendary giant-killers. now
the future is gaining on us, laughing at our
distress, our outsourced obsolescence.

fatal verdicts of pot-bellied robot bwanas
are photocopied, filed. i try to remember
my name, some fundamental principle.
i'm sorry et cetera, if only dot com.

24

one night i woke up in tibor's bathtub, my
heart bursting with joy, embarrassing
sideburns like a founding father, the
stars trembling in fugitive anticipation.

those wild nights and acrobatic days, i didn't
just dream it all, they were real: supermen
caught us when we fell, all flowers were
fires and people only lied in the movies;

the sun stood still for a day and dorothee
stood at the top of the stairs, waiting for
me in high heels and ketchup stains;
bernard hermann soundtrack, gioconda smile.

Hair on Fire

still not quite a model citizen,
'too careless' i'm told,
looking for a short cut
like a former child star
crying his eyes out
for a comeback
or pressing my feet
into the wet sand
the local sun frying
my brain drowning
me in light it's like
the last time i got
tasered, hair on fire
and world war 3s
glittering behind my eyes.

Man of the Year

'The Two Faces of Superman!' Superman #137,
May 1960

our bloody superman
takes a bow,
peeps on the hotties
with his x-ray vision.

hard to smile,
kryptonite
could be
anywhere. he
found a cure
for aging, squeezed
coal into diamonds,
pretended it didn't
hurt when we forgot
to say thank you.

the nerd in the howdy
doody mask yelling
been there done that.

confusing dreams
of alien life forms.

the motiveless hate
of the super-villains.

snowballing echoes in
his bachelor apartment.

Cadences

bad habits, smirking behind the curtain,
your hair in a bob, who could forget,

stratocumulus ugly and ill-tempered,
shared foggy mornings by the bay,

hours—empty rusty buckets of them
--drifting merrily down the stream,

why can't you just give it to me straight
you said, missing my point entirely,

you and your singsong style of phrasing
turning truisms into questions, granite

into sand, here i am playing catch-up,
taking notes, waking up in the park,

counting hollow-bone birds and magic
words, re-arranging the props,

our things and the words for them,
meaning what they say; no more.

Follow The Leader

on cannon street east no on ever changes.
we stay who we are. tibor, potty-mouthed
cherub. feeble fickle darrell hanging round
the crossroads. dad, his gentle regrets of a
life in sales. kindersluts looking for a ride.
rebel angels in goth gear. so it goes. we
play out the roles our parliamentarians
have decreed, double-check the name
tags, memorize the cue cards with a
jaunty sort of apathy. something about
wounds and the fear of wounds dictate
our postures, our pleasures that just leave
us hungrier. between blinks, occasional
images of a mythic prairie town where
a litter of kittens is front page news,
chinooks hammer down like God's fists
and gary cooper's still on the marquee;
tight-lipped, checking the clock, counting
his friends down to zero, waiting for the
noon train that will decide everything.

A Blue Jay Died on my Balcony

and that was it. how much of this world,
its comings and goings, flicker and fade
unnoticed, unremarked upon, it scared me,

i stayed up watching infomercials: chocolate
pasta makers, cancer cures, magic blenders.
jupiter and saturn collided and we didn't even

look up, just watched the highlights on tv and
passed the popcorn. that was the last straw.
i stole a truck, i changed my name, i hoped

it would help but nobody even blinked an eye.
you said who cares, turn up the volume, but
the world is not an illusion, kathy; you are.

they're replacing the mysteries with generic
replicas, halos of fire with styrofoam rings,
fathers and friends with b-move bit players,

i recognize this guy from a disney sunday
night movie--what was i, six? odd to be so
moved by a haunted lighthouse, the whisper

of buried treasure. odd the things you never
forget, clutching at words and names and
priceless things on a planet gone plastic.

Against The Dawn

sleeping with the radio on.
the dream of flying bicycles,
pentecostal as a rainbow.

tearful goodbyes at infinity's
train station. celebrity cameos.
protean shadows dancing in

the fallow fields. blink--time
to reapply the mask. the
mirror is waiting for you.
the daily reunion of language

and mouth. we awake into
forgetfulness, choke on the frost,
wave our resumes like the tattered
flags of time-buried republics.

Angry Candy

go-getters, hard-chargers
laying it on the line,
doubling down and
hogging all the overtime,

pushing too hard too soon,
planning for the future--
and others who don't even
resist: they give in to the

devil, his angry candy.
souls like bent coins
in hell's slot machine,
pink slips, bills, voices

that molt into air raid
sirens drowning out
the self-help guru's
yadda yadda yadda.

Planting Rainbows

foraging among
the *terra incognita,*
the polar opposite
of wherever you are,
carving boomerangs
in the outback, pumping
gas in the shadow of the
pyramids or planting
rainbows in fritz lang's
metropolis, maybe. the
phony b-movie backdrop
dots the i for me, imagine
frost in july, no sir no
exchanges without a
receipt, or a persistent
muscular twitch that
reminds you of the
hour in which you
really blew it.

On Wearing A Tie

1

among those bankrupted pizza joints
security cameras and sitcom reruns

how much lost unfound time the
inescapable geometry of it all

as the ghost of a b/d/s/m hooker
screamed into her cell phone

'what do you mean i gotta walk?'

2

so i shivered on a slippery pew
stuttered out a prayer waited

for something to happen
the world and its contents

spelled out in old-school
fonts bold-face letters at

least it was a start maybe

3

easter came so late that year
i had almost given up

almost forgotten what it's like
the first bloom the new leaves

a cure for aging the irresistible
sweetness of it all and why

would you want to fight it anyhow

4

i started wearing a tie
i wanted to look classy

i liked how it brought out
the blood in my eyes

you said i looked like a waiter
but with that kind of smile

you might have been joking

5

nobody recognizes me,
i wonder if they ever had, or—

no more questions, apes in
fancy shoes, frantic, they've

never even heard of dorothee
as they casually shove past

me in the express lane.

Pick A Letter

homeless guy no. 3
asks pedestrians if
they're saved. my
former better half

goes overboard on
the nytol. you cheat
at scrabble solitaire,
wear a mask to hide

your mean streak as
thunderclouds throb
like tumors. some cop
gave a veteran a ticket

for loitering and an ant
ran away with my bagel.
i'm shopping for houses
in the country just so i

can say goodbye and
good luck to you, with
your fistful of consonants
and your q without a u.

For A Good Time Call

multitasking, alphabetizing my failures while
vacuuming the stairs, willie nelson reminds
me of dad's rural graces, the way he stopped
smiling after the expropriation. this one's
for him. or for billy the kid; a bullet from
your best friend is no way to go. i never
seem to choose, it's getting ridiculous,
i'm sure part of me is missing but the
x-ray was inconclusive, that smudge
could have been a fly, or a bee. inside
the hive, a bee tells his life story by
shaking his ass. the stinger's just for
show, he'd rather dance, royal jelly
smeared on his jaws. i'm jealous, i
can't sting or dance or slam dunk
and the dating agency returned my
deposit. applicant has strong opinions
about art and politics, turns invisible
at odd times, enjoys sleeping in late,
running from success and swears adam
west is still history's best batman. that
one's a deal-breaker, don't even ask.

Novelty Gift Shop, Limeridge Mall

i was looking for
a jigsaw puzzle,
nothing fancy—
wind-up rabid teddy bear,

potty-mouthed santa claus.
jesus action figure with
king fu power punch,
whoopie cushions.

naked-lady playing cards,
elevator-muzak version of
'welcome to the jungle.'
leering dog-faced boy

behind the cash register:
no refunds, no exchanges.
pink florescent light bulbs,
burning out or else too bright.

Military Mind

i'm the designated driver again, fuming listening
to boozy rants re: star wars and the female organ.
the day, bleeding out, fading like a lover receding
from view and no one, not one of us, knows what
to do next. whistling zeppelin, somebody's sister
starts to dance all alone, raises up an elbow like
a dorsal fin before diving into the murky depths:
her skirt is very short, her tattoo is chinese for
'patience.' just imagine for the sake of argument
my brain was full of toy soldiers, the kind you
saw on the backs of old comic books, millions
of them restaging the great battles: normandy,
thermopylae, stalingrand, okinawa, gettysburg.
suddenly the generals have a coup on their hands;
the grunts are tired of taking all the risk, the lousy
food. an a-bomb, an a-bomb, quoth alexander the
the great, my kindgom for an a-bomb. can we go
now? there's a bill i have to pay tomorrow; maybe
i'll write myself a little note. something's missing,
it's so obvious, i'd like to talk about it but like a
boot on the neck silence pretty much says it all.

Watching the Regatta

dragon boats slice through the water like machete blades.
the rowers are so lean, so military, it's sad they'll have
to grow up some day. in 1000000 b.c., when i was in
high school, i never tried out for the rowing team, the
football team, the chess team,--i never tried, period.
some things never change, as you are oh so quick to
remind me. black cherry for you, strawberry for me,
melting down waffle cones faster than we can eat. in
spite of myself it's hard not to get swept up as the kids
near the finish line, we're standing now, cheering for
the orange team even as the blue team edges up and
beats them by a photo-finish. i knew i really loved
you when you said sometimes love isn't enough.
that was wednesday. today is sunday, the first day
of some new chapter, inconclusive and grim. i
only recognize happiness by its absence, after
the fact (the echo on the stairs, the coat hangers
tinkling in the closet), maybe that means i'm
happier now than i think i am, and wouldn't that
just be the icing on top of my turd-flavored
birthday cake? the winners bow their heads,
receive their medals in the queen's gazebo.
canada geese make their mark, squawk and
crow and strut around like they rule the world
four months before they're christmas dinner for
overstuffed aldermen with no idea what hunger is.

The Mongol Invasions

i have as of late acquired the ability to
turn myself into fictional characters,
it's an old man in a rent-controlled
basement today—no one suspects
he's really an eccentric billionaire
with a thousand years of memories.
i prowl the malls, laugh at the
baffled cluelessness of the
bargain-hunting taxpayers.
i seem to recall having
magic powers, a dozen
wives and x-ray eyes;
watching atoms knit
themselves into pairs,
then clans, then faces.
maybe a face will say
hi to me today, maybe
i'll make a new friend
who truly understands:
we'll trade war stories
about missing dorothee
and rampaging across
asia with genghis khan.

No Sweat

scrubbing mildew off the bathroom tiles
it's hard not to wonder
about the miniature armageddons
being acted out in the neighboring cages,
the variegated forms of lust and pity,
the so-called living rooms,
the marathon runner
too dehydrated for tears.
a monosyllabic curse
crawls in under the door.
'i could have been a v.i.p,
a captain of industry, if it
wasn't for you, you, you.'
like a creepy idiot savant,
hamilton ontario canada
is awesome and oblivious
and no help at all: should
i apologize on bloody knees,
or join a traveling circus?
it would be easier if it was
a math problem, robotically
unambiguous, no sweat,
just integers, fractions,
and negative numbers.

Alarm Clock

flesh, is what i say
to me, falling through
the black hole,
opening my eyes,
instantly drowning
in lusts and goals
and himalayan
mountain ranges
of relentless flesh.
a narrow path through the garden,
eyes that see the invisible—
no, not today. catch a bus,
work overtime and rent a movie.
so much for the still small voice
and what was that dream
trying to tell me? who
dreamed the dream
and gave it to me?

Sirens

the cars, their pistons complicit with my appliances,
bleat out a song, atonal and cold. i get the message.

the skittering sound under the fridge, the clicking
in the heart of the toaster tag-team me into

submission. you said you'd stay if i tried to change
but the world's too round for that nonsense; no one

changes except on tv. across the street blinds are
drawn, blue HD light spilling out of the cracks.

a 737 swings around the block waiting for a runway.
the future's hum keeps me up all night; when i sleep

i will dream of america, her cowboys and spacemen,
her vast western lands, her pixellated kisses frozen

in celluloid. after awhile you get sick of fighting it.
machines in sleep mode sleep with one eye open.

the song swells. all our hard drives join the chorus.
it sounds like a song i'd forgotten a long time ago.

After What Used To Be

running from thalidomide to viagra
a sci-fi voodoo blurs the words
of old *hamilton spectators*
and smug ex-genocidaires
hiding behind forged papers.
amid tin mills gone ghostly,
the slag heaps still glow
with a regretful nostalgia.
frantic thought-police rush
to meet their monthly quota.
it's hard to keep up with all
the new rules: even miracle
must follow strict safety
by-laws. still i recall your
hair like an avalanche of
gold, jokes, toys, knees bent
in febrile supplication, the
mystic covalence of digit and
pudenda, the man who tasted
colors and that time you said
relax man—eyes laughing—as
you sipped at steaming chinese tea.

Heroes

decisive men of action are my heroes:
steve reeves in a badly-dubbed
swords-and-sandals epic,
robert mitchum sneering
'baby i don't care,' and
whoever it was who
invented zippers. me,
i'm more like the alienated
parisian pickpocket talking
with his hands, waiting for
the knock on the door, the
ride downtown, the ink on
the fingertips. forks in the
road make me panic like
a rabbit. i should stop
imagining a masai hut
in tanzania as a kind of
utopia, with nothing to
say and a different wife
for every day of the week.
i want to let it all go, i
want to snore on martin's
couch after everybody's
gone home, change my
name and start over,
travel on a fake passport
as dust motes like stars
tell me what happens next.

Common Knowledge

there are some things everybody knows.
hard word pays off, except sometimes.
most leprechauns are pervy peeping
toms. don't mix whites and colors.
you're as old as you feel, unless
you're dead, in which case silence
is golden. in a pinch duct tape can
save your life. angel feathers cure
crohn's. they lied to us; the future
was supposed to me more jetson-y.
and the way stars loomed larger
in black and white, when the men
wore hats and called every female
'baby.' the way stars only seem to
twinkle; it's really just a trick of
the eye. every year winter takes us
by surprise, makes us look like
dummies, like reptile-brained
instinct-machines. opportunity
knocks. the wolf is at the door.
this is someone's good old days,
as we doze through ben-hur on
blu-ray and judgment day paces
at stage left like starter wife
#2, grinding her teeth and
just beginning to keep score.

A Moment of Sincerity

queen takes pawn, the isotope's half life crackles on
the dog frequencies, the END IS NIGH guy quotes

revelation to oblivious retired chessmasters and i can't
read with the wind whipping at these pages. i know

how it ends already: the good guy wins, or vice versa.
either way, i'm happy, a little thirsty. i love this park,

its broad brushstrokes, its guano-stained statue of empress
victoria, her perennial widow's weeds, she would've

dubbed every puddle in the world lake albert if she'd
thought they'd let her. tim preaches determinism

even as every flutter of pulse is freighted with an
electric significance. this breeze tastes...holy.

this book is overdue, a buck twenty in late fees. the
world so densely packed, cocky, cool, a pointillist

master dapples our shapes in a coat of bloody photon,
you notice, it all clicks—autonomic reflex, figures of

speech, arc of a smile—and between heartbeats,
between the seasons, i mean every word i say.

Mind Your Manners

your life's all parking lots now. friends
die off and leave you holding the bag,
with no way home and clown shoes
on your feet. the jagged rock beat
that explained everything, it's
just noise, no soulmates or
angels, only masked strangers
and robots gone uppity. the
saw-toothed palm reader
talks of fame and friday's
winning horses, artfully
dodges the hows and whys.
her crystal ball throbs like
a baleful enraged eye. is
this it? is this what you were
looking for when you went
out looking for a pizza?
don't laugh, sit up straight,
and don't forget to kiss the
monkey on your way out.

A Sort Of Penance

miscellaneous enchantments to boost
one's confidence or repel super-villains:
a radioactive meteorite or a magic word,
for example. the faces you wear. parking
lots to the horizon in mississauga ontario.

all hail lord dracula, in sunglasses and
sunscreen, saying, 'i don't tan, i burn.'
birds know something we don't know,
it's all you can do to curse the mocking
sticky gravity of downtown thursdays.

constellations contort themselves into
advanced yoga poses as mom drives
in circles looking for a parking spot.
where are we? and who carved that
wrinkle when your back was turned?

it all escapes you, even your shoe size.
you're too busy mentally reviewing,
as a sort of penance, all the goofy tv
shows you watched as a kid, before
you were old enough to know better.

Her Majesty

dorothee walks like a queen
(atoms fuse in her wake), she
doesn't even know she's doing it.

i woke up crying from
a dream starring a guy i
haven't seen since 1987
--why?

he had a secret but wouldn't
tell, a wooden horse turned
into a rocket ship, this bus
transfer expires in 45 minutes.

Shell Game

you can even change the names if you want to.
you can build a life out of toothpicks,
pretend it's all a joke. funny the hells
our dream-homes become, black holes
under the sink and cerberus pissing
on the lawn. it's not that you don't
care about your co-worker's cat,
you're just weak from dreaming
of childhood, that vacation to the
florida keys. and the panhandlers
who see what the winners don't,
our decay disguised as progress
like a cosmic bait-and-switch.
you thirst, you long for a love
strong as death, limitless and
wild like jupiter's great red
spot, like the world's first
flowers, standing tall as
if frost was just a rumour.

Common Elements

narcoleptic fogs swaddle the suburbs
until no one dreams and stupidity's
ubiquity rivals that of hydrogen.

i thought i'd figured things out until
i heard of a fish that's 97% water,
thinner than this page, translucent

as the family ghost. stage left,
icthyosaurs laugh at us. pity
the man with a hi-def screen

for a head. his neural nets co-opted
by hollywood, tweets and likes
form a web, an electric amnion.

what to say about such a man? he's
frightened of a verdict, now, for
instance, or after his death.

Dirty Bomb

oceans away in God's name
the strong boiled the weak
with garlic and olive oil.

you clawed at your gadgets,
texted and sexted on i-pads
etc. like a mantis on meth.

holy sunday ended with a
field goal, supermodels
kissed their superhero

husbands. later: garbage
disposal, plasma tv, a cat
caught in a tree, dreams

of tabloid stars, 'same as
it ever was.' birds were
the first to notice, then

the dogs. the perpetrator
remained anonymous.
the virus went airborne:

symptoms included fever,
lycanthropy, vampirism,
cannibalism, and finally

the urge to jump out high
windows, arms flapping,
reaching in vain for the

other side of the clouds,
the moon, the heaven no
one believed in anymore.

Learn Your Lesson

acne-scarred teenagers laugh at my
funny hat, my threadbare tuxedo,
but don't you dare: you know better.

i'm your minimum-wage jiminy cricket,
the ringleader of the circus you live in.
you know the routine: you're here to

learn a lesson, and time is something
you don't have. you can lie to your
mother but not to me, or maybe you're

just dreaming it all. carnival barkers
with loaded dice. coffins of memory,
the soulmate you never met. the film

noir detective agency. rain tapping on
the glass like skeletal fingers. the blind
man tiptoeing through the hall of mirrors.

Good Reasons

people frighten me, sunshine does too,
the way it pours so inexorably through
the cracks in the brickwork, the slits
between the rafters. i'm always in
motion, i have no choice, mr. kapatia
taught us that in grade ten physics
when headbanger or jock was the
fatal ultimatum and we held our
breath waiting for world war 3.
gravity compels me, that's why
i walk a mile for a shwarma at
3 a.m., leave pennies in random
mailboxes, remake the book of
exodus as a mythical western
starring randolph scott, he was
so battered, so resolute in ride
the high country (1962), with
bit parts for all those lost men
spurring their horses toward
freedom and away from the
civilized pieties of straight-a
students. the important things
don't get said, you store them
up in an ornate antique box,
mermaids stenciled in gold
dust on the lid. the strong and
weak nuclear forces give me
a headache, that's why i lied
about avatar etc. i'm naked,
guilty, without excuse, that's
why i drove all day to surprise
you with peaches, that's why i
kissed your clavicle so intensely.

Purgatorio

after church a crashing junkie curses me for smiling.
she's lost things; i've lost things. the year's last
leaves bleed from green to red. a prayer just won't
come.
the tap drips like a countdown to God knows what.
i check under the bed for dust bunnies and vampire
bats.

To-do List

i wouldn't call it a plan. check the news,
the dictator death pool, the weather—

u.s. steel's been spraying rust against the
sky's canopy, the occult slag-flavored

spots on our lungs spawn with a martial
frenzy--the job bank, i'm either under-

or over-qualified—talk about luck! walk
to the end of the pier, say hello to france.

coax the day into ripping off her mask,
she's such a tease, playing the best

movies when i'm sleeping, de-listing the
ex's phone number, bathing us in pixel

until we breathe through our mouths and
can't see ourselves in mirrors. dream.

i'd love to go back in time and un-invent
half the world; we got a little bit carried

away after edison. stop. the little stick man
says so. go. past the carlton inn, heads

bent over beers, a-rod strutting on the big
screen. past the abandoned blocks, the

brown fields. out past the condos, the new
opera house we'll never stop paying for.

On Waking in Someone Else's Bed, Someone Else's Clothes

old iron bells ring out and if i could remember my name
i still wouldn't bother, i'd pick someone else to be, a
warlord of mars, a prehistoric barbarian, a romantic
spy with a suitcase full of secrets and a femme fatale
waiting for me in the fog. gloria grahame, please, if
ava gardner's busy. my head hurts, i'm surrounded
by stuffed animals: garfield and kermit and others i
don't recognize. no clocks tick: it's the future; we're
digital. i'm wearing a miami dolphins jersey, i hate
sports and if i was eastern orthodox i would speak
of theosis by which we become a new species,
partakers of the divine nature, i'd like to believe
but faith is in short supply ever since the embargo,
i remember that much. every bed has its own
unique set of markers, sets and subsets of
tints and tones determined by the history of
its component parts and the dream diaries of its
owner: i really must be going. hard to believe
i don't remember you. your freckles remind me
of the constellation cassiopeia. your skin tastes
like limes. a gentle helix of steam rises from
the oolong chai. i'm going to be late for work.

Darrell Epp

Work

blue collar labour, loading trucks
and some trains, tightening bolts,
painting barns, slinging chains.
they didn't even have to pay me,
i was so happy to be someplace
where thinking was superfluous,
discouraged, even. we got paid
by the hour, counted the minutes
until lunch time while the rest of
the world ran for its life. a tactical
retreat, a capitulation to weakness,
time's inexorability, uncollected
litter, sports cars crowned with rust.
life, all of it, a sort of pantomime
in the dark, an urgent refusal to
face adulthood's painful truths:
receding gum lines, the ghost
that haunts itself, christmas
cards to which i never reply,
your song, love's iffy alibis.

Souvenirs Of Who Knows What

the oceans in your eyes.

dusk, rolling in like the
last saturday in pompeii.

a fortune cookie saying
'you cry at weddings,
you laugh at funerals.'

a fortune cookie saying
today just isn't your day

it's all downhill from here
you screwed it up

a broken jukebox in the
best burger joint on mars.

your enemy in the mirror,
limbs jerking robotically
like a marionette with
tangled strings. a stop
sign that means more
than just 'stop'--we awoke
from a dream in its shadow.

the stop sign still grieves,
puts on a black veil every
april fool's day. a necklace
of vampire teeth and whole
wardrobes knitted out of
secrets, not because i like
secrets but just because
nobody ever asked me.

Invisible Engines

for sentimental reasons i cartwheel around the bay,
overturn rocks, poke at squirming earthworms.
should i call dr. doom, or mom? pray for a
miracle, or a check in the mail? 'normal'
would be so nice, like a bubbling jacuzzi.
(i act out barbie-and-ken kitchen-sink
dramas with your voodoo dolls when
i tire of stabbing at them, sniff at your
junk mail like a randy bloodhound.) a
bit of sun cascades down coniferous
branches as i not-pray to no-one. an
oil tanker is swallowed up by the
horizon. at night the world's edges
are less defined, it all blends together
into a monochromatic stew. ducks
and geese patrol the yacht club,
gliding along the green-glass water
without seeming to move a muscle;
all the real action's under the surface.

Lazy

'this present moment'
dies before you've
finished saying it

the whitewater rush of life,
it's something to think about,
although thinking about it
doesn't seem to do much good—

dorothee just walked in and said,
shouldn't you be working?

On Baldness

i lick her fingers i scrub the pan but
i've never exceled at multitasking
that's why things take me so long
i'd thought i'd be famous a decade
ago or at least before i went bald
like a trappist monk those monks
keep busy idle hands are the devil's
playground they make cheeses and
beers trappist beers improve with
age no one ever said that about me
not even the owner of said fingers
these are the last days so i turn from
the dirty dishes to the face of beauty
oh how i miss her when she travels
to ottawa when she checks the mail
she's so pretty it's deafening what
is she saying something about the
recycling bin the overdue library
books different coloured outfits
and the sorts of shoes that match
them and hurry up please it's time.

Water Up To My Knees

wet surf pulses between my toes a catfish
glares up at the uninvited guest muddying

up his dinner table a jet-ski scares away
geese ducks seagulls and even swans as

i remember with surprise my grade three
teacher who gave me a week's detention

for my low math scores even after i told
her look math just isn't my thing but she

felt insulted vengeful she screamed i was
scared and eventually sorry for her and her

wasted efforts and i did figure math out
eventually it just took awhile. now the jet

ski is almost gone the birds will be back
they were here first someone waded in

this marsh in 1916 1816 1716 176 and
it feels nice to be a part of something.

Good Advice

it took awhile, but i finally learned
to sit quietly in my room, as blaise
pascal so wisely recommended:
after awhile it's just like riding a bike.
inexorably, my big ideas are tossed
in the recycling bin. a crater looms
behind each one of us, a vastness we
wear like the mark of cain. thoughts
become a series of gems in algebraic
sequence, forming a spiral staircase.
when the frost carves capillaries on
the window i go out and pull funny
faces at the raccoon under my car.

Telephone Game

the message ran around the world; by the
time it came back to me i had a wooden
leg and lived in a castle made of bone.

my pet unicorn could sing like a bird.
i was a wanted man, one step ahead
of irs, kgb and other sinister acronyms.

i beat superman at arm-wrestling and
punished all who loved me. love's a
word poets use as a crutch, like 'very'

and 'and.' funny how love brought out
my inner martyr; a lesser man would
have broke both your arms. what was

it, that thing you thought you wanted?
sorry. but don't look at me, look at the
universe, downright peacock-y in its

nightly burlesque: supernovae like
popped corks; the milky way,
waving her spiral arms like shiva

herself; the gravity that pulled me
to you, indiscriminate, affirmative, it
felt like heaven, or the next best thing.

Suicide

to me, these suicide chicken wings
contain more monumentality
than the mons olympus mountain
on mars, 15 miles high and
wider than arizona

shirtless on the patio, licking
my fingers and not thinking of
anything, not even dorothee or
payday. i love it, they're never
too spicy and i never get enough:

the good thing about not having
friends is not having to share.
the woozy dusk is full of fireflies,
swaying like sentimental drunks
under stuttering star fields of neon.

New Wrinkle Found On The Face On Mars

that's big news for sure, but i just keep on typing,
thinking about a peach i bit into when i was ten,
sticky juice ruining my shirt, the hall of mirrors
gimmick that butts in when i try to explain: the
closer i get, the further you run...the robot rover
digs for core samples, pockmarking the face with
boring holes like acne scars, we won't stop until
he's strip-mined and fracked and why, all he ever
did was smile. planets were somehow sturdier
when they were imaginary. salute the starving
child who has to pay for all our pointless nerdy
excursions. here's another news flash: my teeth
hurt, we're always tripping over clues and when
i pick up the phone i swear i can hear the ocean.

Science Says

i dreamed i was happy. then a raccoon started
pulling on a loose shingle, the sound of
those claws like a dead man on my chest.
i went downstairs, told the robot to set
up the chessboard and boil me an egg.
thought about tolstoy, churchill, our
heroic dead. (i loved you more than life!)
the droid was supposed to help with the
loneliness; i'd better check the warranty.
science says reality's infinite and slightly
curved; that's a fancy way of saying i'll
see you around. some unruly quarks
arrive before they leave. the ground
feels steady but we're really arcing
six different ways at once. is light
a particle or a wave? yes. nothing
is destroyed, everything dies. the
droid checked me, killed my rook,
i never noticed the northern lights,
the sad generous beauty i bathed in.

Immunity

occasionally they change the goal posts
when they think no one's watching.

romances fizzle, red means go, my
parking spot's gone and i'm too

stunned by your ghost—
its cruel zombie-master-like

grip on my thoughts—to even
lift a finger. souls like uhf test

patterns, stars burning through
the periodic table on their way

to the graveyard, lives less heroic
than we'd been hoping for. i give

nairobi a try. the wild women, the
crazy drivers, they seem immune

to it all. i ask them their secret, they
just laugh, ask if white boys are

born with the camera attached. habari
gani? muzuri, always muzuri. through

the gauze of the mosquito net, jacaranda
blossoms are fuchsia, erotic, and seem to whisper.

Peek-A-Boo

humid, ironic, the sky's a bouillabaisse
about to turn. the western wind,
snowball-like, gaining mass

as it rolls down the escarpment.
spinsters weeping over leo in
titanic, men like petrified wood,

dreading the income tax,
playing the lotto like
scratching an itch.

the hidden rebar and wires,
the world's network of veins
and capillaries expressing

itself as a pulse fluttering in the
belly. a miracle of sun, like God's
eye peeping over the radio tower.

Song for the Buffalo

a jumpy teen, drowning in testosterone,
yells *'whachoo lookin' at?'* say nothing,
think of witty replies all the way home.
later, in the dark, add them all up, the
missed chances, mistakes and myriad
misfires, coming up again with some
negative number's square root. they
march on thunderously like america's
ghost herds of buffalo, the dust clouds
of their hooves visible from two states
over. we took the skins for boots and
belts, left the bodies to rot in the sun,
thirty million buffalo corpses in less
than a decade. 'well when you put it
that way...' i want to touch whatever
my father touched, catalogue every
atom, every tinkertoy molecule. i
want to run across the great plains
all the way to the ocean. i want to
stop, reconnoiter, get my bearings
from the stars, smother my rage,
bend down, face close to the loam,
overcome by my desire, my need,
to plant a flower, or to pluck one.

Faux Pas

like the time i said
get lost to that mutant
vagabond asking for

dimes with tears in his
eyes only to realize
with a shock it was

just me, staring into
the mirror-glass facade
of the nation's largest bank.

Does This Ever Happen To You

the complaint department burned to the ground
and i had no plan b. who to tell, who to see,

about the punk ghost spraying graffiti across
my junk dna, life's bogus causalities, this

face that reminds me of lee marvin not at all?
i've always thought the alphabet needed more

letters, maybe something between the q and the r,
a bantu click a glottal stop, a phlegmy growl

from deep in the neck—and the mad scientist
is running late, he promised me results back

in the clinton years and i'm sick of waiting. all i
want is to break down the world into its parts

and reverse-engineer a place slightly saner, safer,
i'd add a bit more grace, mix up a new color

every hour, mistakes would be less irrevocable...
the space aliens were supposed to be a lot cuter,

most of them don't even pay taxes! paint peels,
a cormorant breaks his wing and we have no

choice so we speak of 'progress' and 'plans'
and 'lisa please, give me one more chance.'

Night Scene

orion the hunter
tightens his belt.

comets and ufo's
scar the inky void.

the radio tower blinks out a
warning to low-flying planes.

somewhere out there a mantis is praying.

canned laughter knocks on my door.

the timeless minutes
i almost slept through:

i get to record it all,
and to whom do i
owe the pleasure.

Toy Soldiers

slapped into submission by the future's
cathode-ray vice-grip, i can't tell the
taxpayers from the ghosts anymore.

the president declares another victory
in the war against the monsters.
no one mentions the transylvanians

freezing in the arctic internment
camps but how i miss my frankenstein
co-workers, the bolts in their neck,

their romantic accents. last week
i had st. vitus' dance, i chipped a tooth,
i called my mom. out by the lake

blonde children play with toy soldiers.
war games are a way of making sense
of the world. the girls feign disinterest

while dreaming of men in uniform.
kathy delivers her weekly ultimatum
as straight-a students bayonet the enemy

right there on the sidewalk, the
purity of their motives somehow
providing an ironclad justification.

One Possible Conclusion

i fell asleep before the story ended.
now i'll never know if the incredible
hulk made it to his therapist in time

to fix his anger management issues,
refill his paxil prescription. so much
rage, incoherent and green. i wish

him peace. i think that's what we all
get in the end, 'current events'
notwithstanding. hints and signals,

one leaf arcing sunward. vertigo.
count all the scars; lock, load. the
world's a fire we all walk through.

where did i leave my game face?
soon the whole gang will be here:

martin, tibor, dorothee, looking for
a laugh and some hot cinnamon cider.

Waiting for an Academy Award

co-workers who should know
a lot better compliment me on
my 'positive mental attitude'
and still no oscar nomination
for 'best impersonation of a
normal.'

i stayed up all night, watching a bumblebee smash
its head into a light bulb. tomorrow should be even more
exciting.

but that's enough about me.

Darrell Epp

Hard To Read

distant thunder. the air i breathe
crackling with electricity.

screaming crows pinned to
the sky like crucified criminals.

hard to read, i stare at the
same sentence for decades--

put the book down, stand,
raise your hands, prepare
to welcome the raging storm.

Steps

what's it like to be a baby?
how did i think before i thought in language?

all the relentless endings and beginnings,
the endless cycle of the seasons, their
births and rebirths, time's headlong march—
i'm not frightened anymore

i know there's a place
i'm traveling to

i know i'll arrive

on time.

After Hours

drunken angels,
tangoing on the
head of a pin.

a bloody dart
poking out of
st. sebastian.

ol' blue eyes
on the radio.
peanut shells

under my feet.
last call never
comes. infinity

hides between
0 and 1. pity
the designated

driver: guardian
angels dance
like st. vitus.

Attention Historians!

attention tenured historians,
the public wearies of your
improbable power fantasies
and dreary morality plays.

skip the norman invasions
and hutterite geneologies
and find room in your
textbooks for the following:

the first cigarette, the last
hotel room, dorothee's
footprints in the snow,

her favourite pajamas,

the lost toys of kindergarten,
the ideal that begat the real,
the things that don't change,
and the words for them.